Twig's Moon

Written by Dana Roffler

Illustrated by Ashley Kenawell

I was lying in bed late
one night with my dog.

My cat was there too and
we all slept like logs.

The night air blew in
through the door in a stream.

And the moonlight
flowed over our heads like a dream.

My eyes jumped wide
open-cat and dog eyes did too.

I rolled out of bed
and put on my left shoe.

Then Bertha the hound dog
and Twiglet the cat

And I became still when
we noticed a bat .

The bat circled our heads then flew out in the night.

Twig, Bertha and I ran to follow her flight.

Moonlight laid a path straight across our big field.

Twig ran out in the lead, Bert and I chased his heels.

An owl hooted twice as we raced
by her pine tree –

First the bat, then came Twig,
then Bertha, then me.

I was running so fast that I lost my shoe.

To stop running to find it
would just never do.

Our brown bat flitted
over a wide woodland stream.

We three flitted too –
on the light of the beam.

We didn't touch foot on a rock or a log.

Though I spied in the water the eyes of a frog.

Twig ran far ahead and he leaped into the air

On the path of moonlight-it shone clear and fair.

Bert and I leaped up too with our feet on the light.

On our way we encountered a Luna in flight.

A lake rippled below as we raced so high

We ran far above it – right up in the sky.

The stars danced in close.
They sparkled and twirled

As we sped on the moon
path high over the world.

Then I stopped and I stood
with my arms around Bert.

Our two hearts were pounding
so hard that that they hurt.

We gazed at the moon,
Twig had paused just in front.

The bat fluttered right in.
We were done with our hunt.

But it wasn't quite over.
One thing happened more.

Twig looked in my eyes
and my heart got so sore

I thought it would
shatter and explode in the sky.

But it stayed where
it was and I'll never know why.

Twiglet blinked then he turned and jumped into the moon.

We tried to follow but a voice said "You're too soon.

It isn't your time . You have to go home.

You and Bert have each other. You won't be alone."

We cried for a while then had to turn 'round

To follow the moonpath back down to the ground .

I looked back one more time and
what did I see ?

Twiglet's face in the moon.
He was smiling at me .

Then Bert grabbed my shirt in
her mouth and we travelled

Over the lake as the
moonpath unravelled.

Over stream and through woods –
the owl was long gone

As we crossed the big field,
the night turned to dawn .

Then somehow we were
waking up in our own bed.

Bert lay right beside me,
my hand on her head.

I went to pat Twig
but his pillow was bare

Except for a whisker – that's all that was there.

We miss our friend Twiglet and we're counting the nights

'Til the next July moon comes up big and bright.

We're sure if we look at the moon for a while

We'll see Twiglet's face and his Cheshire cat smile.

The author of this story is Dana Roffler. She is the caretaker of the cats at Ralphie's Retreat. Her home is next to the shelter and she resides with twelve cats and two dogs. She also wrote Firefly Ball (available on Amazon) to help support her shelter family.

Ashley Kenawell, besides being an artist, and the illustrator of this book, is the foster mother of Moss and Bethany. Moss and Beth were Ralphie residents for fourteen months.

Profits from this publication go to Ralphie's Retreat, a shelter dedicated to the care of Feline Leukemia positive cats. This shelter is located in western Maine. Ralphie's Retreat opened in July 2013. Our cats have come to the Shelter from Maine, Massachusetts, Vermont, New York and Delaware.

The impetus to create RR was a cat from East Boston, Ralphie and his probable offspring Gabriel – both strays. Gabe was trapped and taken to a clinic for treatment. The clinic tested him for Feline Leukemia before treating him. His test was positive for the disease and the clinic euthanized him and THEN called to tell us this.

RR gives FeLV+ cats a chance to live their lives in a loving, safe, sunny environment. They are treated with Western medicine and Alternative medicine. We place cats in foster care when appropriate. We currently house seven cats and have seven cats in foster homes. Our plan is to expand the Shelter to house cats with Feline Immunodeficiency Virus and cats with both FeLV and FIV.

We are on facebook. Thanks for your support!

Made in the USA
Charleston, SC
09 June 2015